*just when the caterpillar
thought the world was over...*

Array of Hope
An Afterlife Journal

Lynda Lee Macken

Published by

BLACK CAT PRESS
P. O. Box 1218
Forked River, NJ 08731

Copyright© 2008 by Lynda Lee Macken.

All rights reserved. No part of this book may be reproduced or transmitted electronically, orally, or in any other fashion without permission in writing from the publisher.
For information please contact
Black Cat Press.

ISBN 978-09755244-5-9

Printed in the United States of America.

Cover design by Deb Tremper, Six Penny Graphics,
Fredericksburg, VA

This book is dedicated to my mother

LIV INGRID

who I will miss until we reunite in the next realm…

A woman of great elegance and style,
she possessed artistic ability and the knack to create
"something out of nothing" – a brilliant alchemist.

LEO 14: CHERUB-LIKE, A HUMAN SOUL WHISPERS INTO EVERY RECEPTIVE EAR, SEEKING TO MANIFEST...

...symbolizes the desire to be heard and taken seriously. This 'Human Soul' is trying to find a 'Receptive Ear,' someone who will listen to what's being said.

There is likely to be a deep realization that will transform your life on some level. Your creative or spiritual aspects are attempting to come through into conscious expression. Listening to your inner voice, along with heeding messages from others, can lead you to the next level of your life.

There is a need to listen to messages now, as something is seeking expression and it needs a vehicle to be able to 'Manifest' it. Perhaps you are the "vehicle?"

Messages from the other side. Channeling information. Spirit descending, wishing to make its self known. Whispering. Passing on news and messages. Seeking embodiment. Transpersonal urges. Cherubs and spirits. Ears and hearing.

— EXCERPT FROM *360 DEGREES OF WISDOM, CHARTING YOUR DESTINY WITH THE SABIAN ORACLE* BY LYNDA HILL

What's with your ears?
— EXCERPT FROM ASTROLOGICAL READING WITH LYNDA HILL

CONTENTS

A Ray of Hope   *1*

Hearing Liv's Voice   *5*

Millions of Flowers   *11*

A Psychic Connection   *15*

"Walk!"   *23*

Liv Steps It Up   *31*

The Reunion   *33*

Dreams   *37*

Phone Calls from the Dead   *43*

The Monroe Institute   *47*

Happy Birthday from Beyond   *59*

Weathering the Winter & Further Signs of Life   *61*

"Now You Can Have Your Life Back"   *65*

"Tell Her I Love Her As Much As She Loved Lucy"   *71*

"Play Track Four for Lana"   *75*

Liv Appears   *77*

I'll Be Home for Christmas   *79*

On Reflection   *81*

'Til We Meet Again   *85*

Liv on her 80th birthday.

A RAY OF HOPE

*Death is nothing else but going home to God,
the bond of love will be unbroken for all eternity.*

— MOTHER TERESA

On a mild October evening I plodded along the cobblestone streets of New Hope, Pennsylvania. The town seemed unusually quiet for a Saturday night. I noticed the local ghost tour making its rounds in the historic and very haunted village.

Reluctantly, I headed toward Farley's Bookshop where for the next two hours I would sign my new book, *Haunted New Hope*, and absent-mindedly listen to readers as they shared their ghost stories. Normally an enjoyable event, these days my feelings ranged from numbness to extreme heartache.

My mother, Liv, had passed away six months earlier and I endured the most gut-wrenching emotional pain I ever experienced. Now that she was gone, I also suffered from a lack of purpose. In my loneliness and sorrow, I felt like *I* was the walking dead.

Ducking into one of the shops to kill more time, my eyes were drawn to a square purple magnet imprinted with the following proverb:

Just when the caterpillar thought the world was over,
it became a butterfly.

That's *exactly* how I felt – I thought my life was over. Yet this quote inspired a ray of hope…

I believe in the supernatural. I've collected ghost stories ever since I was a kid. I've witnessed apparitions which motivated me to chronicle true ghost stories in five states. I have appeared on radio and television to share my experiences and also consulted with television producers regarding ghostly phenomena.

Never did I think that I would one day write about post-mortem visits from my mother. In fact, I didn't think I would ever pen another word, that's how disheartened I'd become.

Even though I've recorded hundreds of stories about hauntings and know spirits pose no threat, I usually find unearthly activity disquieting.

My mother played an active role in my regional ghost book publishing venture. Actually, as she lay dying I implored Liv not to haunt me! I was only joking, even though it occurred to me she might.

A friend of mine ultimately witnessed my mother's spirit. I would love to see Liv, but she doesn't think I could handle her appearance. I think I could. But more on that later...

For two years I've enjoyed my mother's after death communications and never once have I been afraid. Liv's continued presence in my life is a transformational gift for which I am eternally grateful.

Array of Hope, An Afterlife Journal presents the many ways my late mother communicated comfort and consolation.

Most of the contact with my mother is *telepathic* – I hear Liv's voice in my mind. This type of transmission was formerly known as "thought transference." Liv's positive and uplifting words helped me to cope with her loss. Hearing her telepathically soothed my grief, accelerated my healing and spurred me on spiritually.

Surprisingly, I also discovered that what I experienced was not so out of the ordinary.

After-death communication is universal and as old as mankind. These subtle contacts are spontaneous, direct and can occur anytime and anywhere; they are extremely common. Actually in many other parts of the world, these spiritual encounters are discussed openly, freely and fondly.

Messages from our loved ones are sacred and profound experiences that are normal and natural. Liv's afterlife communications impelled me to confront my deepest questions about mortality and the soul's survival.

My intent in sharing these stories and extraordinary events is to help others cope with their loss, heal their grieving hearts, and offer a deeper understanding of life after death.

HEARING LIV'S VOICE

Your greatest trial is your greatest triumph.
— NEALE DONALD WALSCH

My mother passed away on March 18, 2006 at 2:35 p.m. on an overcast Saturday afternoon. She lived to be 85 years old, just 16 days shy of her 86th birthday.

My brother Jack and I were present. Wracked with sobs, I knelt beside Liv, held her hand and cradled her head until her heart stopped beating and she peacefully drew her last breath.

Although I believed I had prepared myself for her death my anguish was agonizing. Anyone who has lost a loved one knows that words cannot describe the acute emotional, mental and physical pain of grief. My heart stung with the pain of sorrow and my entire being *ached*. The idea I would never see Liv again was excruciating.

This thought elicited an unbearable emptiness and created a void that rendered life pointless.

The morning after her passing I sat writing a letter to my mother that I wanted placed in her coffin. Composing what I believed to be final words to Liv was agonizing. As I poured my heart out I *heard* her say "Cut it out, will you?" (My mother didn't care for sentimentality). Even though Liv was talking to me from beyond the grave, my grievous stupor prevented me from comprehending this remarkable phenomenon.

When I viewed my mother's body prior to her desired cremation, Liv's expression looked joyous! "You made her smile" I gasped to the funeral director. He shook his head and claimed he didn't do a thing. I knew I made the right decision to see my mother one last time. I felt *so* relieved because through her countenance Liv conveyed to me her happiness.

Even though Liv seemed happy *I* was far from being okay. Not only was my heart shattered, I strained my back getting out of bed. I was a woman without hope in terrible physical pain. Prone on the couch crying uncontrollably I contemplated Liv's photo.

"I'm fine! I'm fine!" I heard her say.

Dealing with my mother's infirmity, the grueling days leading up to her passing and ultimately the finality of Liv's death left me in a trance-like state to say the least. For days I heard Liv's words but *finally* I took pause; her spellbinding statements penetrated the miasma of my grief and I began to wonder… Could my dead mother *really* be talking to me? Since she's fine, *where* is she? *Where* did she go? *How* is she doing this?

In my heart of hearts, I *knew* Liv was talking to me! This was *real!* "I'm fine! I'm fine!" I heard her emphatically exclaim. The unprompted words were in Liv's vernacular – *surely* this was her voice.

This was not the first time Liv talked to me telepathically. As my mother lay unconscious,[1] her breathing and heartbeat slowly diminishing, a nurse

---

[1] Humanity is currently experiencing a consciousness revolution; researchers report awareness in comatose patients.

arrived to assess Liv's condition and lingered in the room. I desperately wanted to be alone with my mother in her final moments. My mother desired privacy also because I *heard* her say, "Why won't she leave us alone? What is she hanging around for? Why doesn't she leave?"

Hearing her words in my head did not faze me – the experience seemed so natural in my surreal state. I didn't give a second thought to the extrasensory perception. I actually found my mother's statements humorous; she continued to gripe and rightfully so.

When my brother arrived to say good-bye, my mother transmitted through me "he smells like cigarettes." I told him what Liv said. He stopped dead in his tracks, possibly because my mother was communicating with me in her comatose condition or maybe because his smoking, which he concealed due to his heart surgery, was exposed.

My sixth sense originated a week earlier after an especially draining Reiki[2] healing circle at the Earth Spirit

---

[2] Reiki is a simple, natural, and safe method of spiritual healing and self-improvement. Effective in helping nearly every known illness, this ancient Japanese technique is beneficial in reducing stress, promoting relaxation, and accelerating healing. It is administered by "laying on hands" and is based on the belief that unseen life force energy flows through all of us.

Metaphysical Center in Red Bank, New Jersey. On that pivotal evening I had symbolically "released" my beautiful mother to the inevitable.

Diagnosed with Alzheimer's disease and congestive heart failure, Liv languished in a nursing home suffering intense pain from four broken bones in her back because of osteoarthritis and osteoporosis. Additionally, she consumed the barest minimum amount of food. Weighing a mere 96 pounds Liv *wanted* to die.

I needed to let her go so I visualized our parting in a peaceful yet tear-jerking, ritualistic way.

During the guided mediation the facilitator led us up a stairway accompanied by our guardian angel. I envisioned the staircase to heaven and imagined my mother with me and my angel slowly climbing the stairs. When moving back down the stairway I left my mother behind. In spite of everything her time drew near and she prayed to go.

In retrospect, I believe the Reiki healing energy opened me up spiritually, heightened my perception and triggered my clairaudient capabilities concurrent with the impending trauma of losing my mother. I suspect these incidents coincided for later in the evening I heard my cats speak to me. I shrugged it off and thought *I guess this is what pet psychics do.*

I am closer to you than you can imagine.
I am always with you.
I love you to infinity and beyond.

We are closer to you than we ever could have been on the earth,
and we will never abandon you.

— EXCERPTS FROM *WALKING IN THE GARDEN OF SOULS*
BY GEORGE ANDERSON & ANDREW BARONE

MILLIONS OF FLOWERS

Let us be silent, that we may hear the whispers of the gods.
— RALPH WALDO EMERSON

After reading dozens of books on the afterlife, I learned that hearing the deceased loved one's voice is normal for the bereaved.

When my brother Jack sold my parents' possessions at a yard sale, a neighbor came by and put aside a few things prior to retrieving her money from home to pay for the items.

"*Give* it to her, *give* it to her," my mother's voice was insistent.

When I told the neighbor that my mother wanted to give her the objects, we both cried a little. I think my brother did too since he missed out on a sale!

Two-way telepathic communication is also possible. In fact it's feasible to enjoy entire conversations this way.

Now that I realized I could talk with my mother, I chatted with her one morning to satisfy my curiosity about the "Other Side." As I relaxed in a meditative state, we shared a revealing exchange...

Lynda Lee: "What was it like to pass over?"

Liv: "It was like nothing. Just there, then here."

LL: "Was there a tunnel?"

Liv: "I don't think so. I don't know. I don't remember."

LL: "What's it like?"

Liv: "Gorgeous. Beautiful. Beyond description."

LL: "Are you happy?"

Liv: "More than happy. I'm ecstatic."

LL: "Who's there with you?"

Liv: "Everyone's here – your father, Mother, Ruth, Knut, Chris, Tom...

LL: "You're free from your body?"

Liv: "That *damn* thing!"

LL: "How is it different from here?"

Liv: "It's glorious."

LL: "What's your favorite part?"

Liv: "The flowers. They're all over. Millions of them! It's heaven. It really is."

LL: "What do you do all day?"

Liv: "We rest. We talk."

LL: "What should people know?"

Liv: "Not to be afraid. It's truly a wonderful place. To love, love, love. That's all there is."

LL: "Are you surprised?"

Liv: "Not really. I kind of knew. Yeah, I guess so."

LL: "You weren't afraid?"

Liv: "No. Not at all."

LL: "Are you coming back?"

Liv: "No. I don't think so. I don't know."

LL: "Any advice for me?"

Liv: "Do your own thing. Don't let anyone tell you what to do."

What a gift! Another time Liv said, "Don't be sad. It's beautiful. It really is. It's spectacular."

A PSYCHIC CONNECTION

There is no death, only a change of worlds.

— CHIEF SEATTLE

By a twist of fate Jean Fellacher of Queens, New York phoned me on the one-year anniversary of my mother's passing; she called to order a copy of *Haunted Long Island*. Usually people don't call me at home to order books. I uncharacteristically engaged her in conversation.

Jean shared she visited several places on Long Island and experienced various paranormal phenomena. For instance while strolling the grounds of Sagtikos Manor in Bayshore she distinctly heard tapping on the window even though the historic site's staff had left for the day.

I mentioned she must be psychic. "I am" she proudly exclaimed. *Now* this woman definitely drew my attention.

Acutely aware I had a psychic on the line on the anniversary of my mother's death, we spoke in general for awhile. Psychic since the age of nine, Jean gives readings on the internet at www.keen.com/psychic and goes by the moniker "Lady Aquarius." She is honest and frank and a third generation psychic.

We shared our opinions about Sylvia Browne and John Edwards. Then she said "You love animals. You care for cats. You feed them, rescue them, shelter them, and you've been doing this for many years."

Indeed. I've maintained a feral cat community for twenty years. "How do you know?" I asked.

"I'm a psychic." Right.

I could hardly believe I held a connection with a psychic on this poignant anniversary – simply astonishing. I don't believe in coincidences; *everything* happens for a reason.

"Do you know a Madeline and a Maryann?"

"Yes." I felt giddy. Madeline and Maryann are Liv's sister-in-law and mine, respectively. In my opinion, these two names would be the *least* likely for my mother to mention. Was Liv being funny? The bottom line is I took notice.

"You wear very little make-up. You're very natural."

As soon as I heard this statement, I *knew* my mother's involvement. Liv always complained I didn't use make-up even as I wore it!

"There's a woman on the Other Side. She's short. Not too thin but yet not heavy. She has curly hair." (My poor mother slept on curlers practically every night of her life!). Jean laughs and says "This is a *very* happy spirit. She's *so* happy." I cry. "Oh my goodness. I've never seen such a happy spirit. She says you were her *rock*."

That did it. Now I'm *certain* Jean is communicating with my mother. Liv always called me her "rock."

Jean said my mother was "no Donna Reed" and called her a woman "ahead of her time." She took no "s-h-i-_!" to put it in the psychic's vernacular. Jean shared my mother was very smart and very funny. "She's *so* funny!" Exactly.

ARRAY OF HOPE

Liv is now <u>very</u> happy spirit!

My mother said there was "no up, no down. No heaven, no hell." "She loves the adventure over there. She's doing *everything*," Jean said.

The psychic mentioned my mother "passed very easily. She wanted to go so badly, and for a long time. She was ready. She felt like a prisoner in her body. An active woman, she liked to do things – keep going. She hated being confined to a bed."

Jean also said "don't be mad at her if she doesn't appear in your dreams for awhile. She's practicing 'tough love.'" "Don't be mad at me" was a phrase my mother often used.

I remained speechless. Here was the perfect chance to speak with my mother yet I couldn't think of a thing to say! Not only was the opportunity unexpected but probably because I remained in contact with Liv and spoke with her many times during the day as we did when she was here in physical form. Finally I asked if my mother would ever appear to me.

"No, because she doesn't think you could handle it. She doesn't want to frighten you."

Liv is probably right. For about a year after her death I felt apprehensive nearly every time I walked into a darkened room in my house or got up at night to go to the bathroom. I kept my eyes closed as much as possible.

Although I wanted to see Liv I never felt the time was right. Yet I know there's no reason to be frightened.

When I witnessed apparitions in the past they were not scary at all. Ever since childhood I've been afraid of the dark. My mother's last words to me were "Keep the living room light on." I do.

The reading I received felt odd because I was used to having my mother in my head and now my focus was on Jean's communication with her – a third party.

Finally I thought of another question for Jean to ask my mother. I wanted to know how she liked the new book I was writing.

"She loves it!" Of course she does, it's all about the post-mortem connection she made with her daughter.

My mother and I share a special bond. I feel all relationships on this earth plane are pre-ordained and I believe we choose our associations prior to incarnating.

Even the current telepathic contact my mother and I share is particularly meaningful.

The time is ripe to recognize our spiritual bonds both in this world and the next. Humanity is evolving rapidly. Our global consciousness is on the rise and interest in mystical and supernatural matters continues to grow.

My mother also imparted, via Jean, that she wanted me to erect lattice-work with rambling roses. My mother cultivated a beautiful rose arbor in our backyard on Staten Island. "But she knows I can't grow roses," I whined.

"Any vine but not grape vines." Knowing her, this was my mother's subtle yet distinctive humor at play.

Jean revealed a lot more information, particulars of a personal nature I prefer not to disclose. There is no way she could know these specifics regarding our family.

"Lady Aquarius" shared amazingly accurate messages. Overall, Jean's reading was strikingly specific; her method gently direct, and did not include "fishing" questions.

Remarkably, psychic connections or *any* form of communication with the Other Side offer us a glimpse into life after death. Also, since psychics receive messages from our loved ones, it suggests we all can directly.

We all possess extrasensory abilities. We follow our "gut" feelings for instance and we can increase our aptitude if we're so inclined.

The next morning my mother and I enjoyed another two-way conversation discussing the serendipity of the psychic's phone call. Here is an excerpt...

LL: "Wasn't that something about the psychic last night?"

Liv: "I planned it."

LL: "It meant so much to me."

Liv: "I know. You needed it."

LL: "I did. Can I talk to you anytime?"

Liv: "I'll be here. Are you losing it?" (I start to cry).

LL: "Yes, I am. Thank you, Liv."

Liv: "I love you, darling."

LL: "I was your rock."

Liv: "I wanted you to know it was me."

LL: "Is Madeline there?"

Liv: "Oh yes. She's beautiful. And your father. He's sad. He's sorry. He's *real* sorry."

"WALK!"

Information comes softly from the natural world.
The seeker must listen carefully to hear the many voices that call.
Listen for whispers from the woods, for wisdom will call.
— SANDRA KYNES

In my grief all I wanted to do was spend time in the woods. "Walk!" was the internal command I heard over and over. Difficult as it was, putting one foot in front of the other became my only goal.

The intuitive knowing to be out in nature was affirmed during a Reiki Healing Circle at the Lifeline Wellness Center in Toms River, New Jersey. As a Reiki practitioner performed the healing treatment she offered I needed to "let go" and spend as much time in nature as possible (!). She stressed again and again I *really* needed to frequent the forest and connect with the natural world in order to effect healing. She also shared I needed to treat myself to a special pair of walking shoes… oddly enough I had purchased an expensive pair the day before!

Fortunately, in the days following Liv's funeral, contractors refurbished my crumbling kitchen and bath in my eighty-year-old cottage in New Jersey's Pinelands. Our "house" is a metaphor for the "self" and the symbolism of having my house/self made over did not escape me. The remodel made everything new again.

The workers' presence forced me out of my home which led me to the special place where I could be alone with my sorrow. I knew I couldn't escape the pain; I needed to go *through* the agony to get over it, if indeed the huge grey cloud engulfing me would ever lift. I *longed* to be in a wooded setting.

While it never came to pass, my mother and I often planned to have a "mountain greenery home" on a lake. Yet I didn't realize just minutes from my house was Eno's Pond County Park where a mile-long nature trail loops through the woods past two observation decks and a duck blind that face the water.

Kingfishers shriek, squirrels scurry, and chipmunks forage. Waxy Indian pipes, wild mushrooms, and pink lady slippers peek through the mossy carpet. Great blue herons soar majestically, snowy egrets wade in the estuary ready to prey, and white-tailed deer gracefully pick their way through the tangle of pines, oaks, sycamores and holly.

Author Eckhart Tolle says birds and flowers are the manifestation of God's love, in his best-selling book, *A New Earth, Awakening to Your Life's Purpose* which I read to pass the dreadfully long days right after Liv's death.

When I discovered the healing paradise right in my own backyard, this time I cried for joy. On a daily basis I spent hours and hours sitting in the sun by the pond, co-existing with the towering trees and enjoying birdsongs. Since childhood I loved being by myself in the woods, yet I never felt alone.

One day I observed a woodpecker, and while marveling at its beauty I heard my mother say "It's a flicker." Right, Liv… I smiled to myself; my mother often corrected my misidentification of birds when she was alive.

The forest is my element; I feel closest to God among nature and in this case I instinctively knew this was where I needed to be in order to nurture and restore my spirit. Mother Nature is the best healer.

During this time an acquaintance flowered into a friendship. Now a retired school principal, Maryann Way and I knew each other for fifteen years. She also lost her mother and she occasionally checked in with me. "Mare" didn't mind that I couldn't get through a conversation without crying.

Quite by surprise I realized I could attain happiness again by reconnecting with things I used to love to do, so I bought a bike – a vintage one-speed bicycle with foot brakes. I loved it! I felt like an eight-year-old again riding around the lakes in my community, relishing freedom and the rushing of the wind.

On her birthday, Mare and I braved a rush-hour bike ride on busy Route 9 to a popular donut shop for breakfast. This was the first of many laughter-filled (mis)adventures we would share.

In an attempt to quell the absorption of calories, we headed to Eno's Park to walk off our donuts. The conversation turned to our mothers' last days.

Mare confided to me that her mother's spirit manifested in her home after she died. She observed her mom as plain as day leaning in the archway with her hand on her hip – her customary pose.

The apparition appeared so real, Mare said, "Hi Mom," without giving it a thought. When she "came to her senses" she looked again but the image was gone.

No sooner were the words out of her mouth, when Mare smelled the distinct aroma of cigarette smoke (we were alone in the park) and felt her mother's presence. Since her mother smoked, Mare took this as a sign. After all, it *was* her daughter's birthday!

Sensing a presence is the most common form of contact for those left behind. Many people discount these experiences thinking it's their imagination. This type of afterlife contact exhibits as a distinct *feeling* that your loved one is close by, yet is not seen or heard. Most typically felt during the days and weeks immediately after death, sensing their presence can occur at any time.

In the days following my mother's passing, I distinctly felt Liv's presence.

One instance transpired when I stopped for coffee at a favorite café and upon entering my car to start the long drive to Gettysburg, Pennsylvania for, ironically, a "ghost conference" I said "I wish you were coming with me, Liv."

"I am" she replied.

I cried uncontrollably during the long, hot weekend. Now opened up psychically, I'm certain my on-going angst was exacerbated due to the collective grief attached to the historic site.

One evening I sat in the subterranean tavern room of the Dobbin Inn which fortunately was lit only by candlelight. As I sat alone at a table for two, tears streamed down my face. I sensed my mother's presence and felt her hand reach across the table to mine. "I wish I knew what to do," she offered.

I frequently discern Liv's presence usually when I'm preparing for company. When alive she often spent time at my house on the week-end and helped me pick up and clean. "It's not that you're dirty" she used to say "but you are messy." My mother was a great cook and we enjoyed working together in the kitchen. Always a great help to me, Liv carries on coaching me regarding tidiness and boosting my confidence when cooking.

During a small gathering at my house, my company gathered 'round the buffet table and admired the hand-embroidered tablecloth.

"Did your mom embroider the cloth?" my friend Susan asked.

I didn't think so. "Probably my grandmother" I answered.

"Ruth did it" I heard my mother say loud and clear. Of course I shared with my guests that my mother just told me Aunt Ruth sewed the design. The look on my friends' perplexed faces was priceless!

Not only is after death contact an extraordinary and spiritual experience, it can be quite amusing.

A few months after Liv's passing, still gripped by sorrow, I sat in my backyard reading *We're Their Heaven* by Allison Dubois, the inspiration for TV's *Medium*. I read about the visits and signs by those who have passed over.

The information meant to comfort, reassure and provide hope left me feeling miserable. My heart was broken, the pain almost too much to bear. I thought *I don't know if I can stand this.*

I cried and cried until I heard my mother say in her imitable way "I think you better stop reading that book."

I started to laugh which lifted me out of my awful funk. Then I heard the lyrics from the song, *Sarah Smile* playing on the radio…

If you feel you can't go on, I'll come and hold you.
It's you, and me, together forever.

Life and death…incredible!

For those that have a genuine interest and a loving heart the doors of knowledge will open.

LIV STEPS IT UP

Death is no more than turning us over from time to eternity.
— WILLIAM PENN

Feeling a touch is another form of afterlife contact. Some feel their hand touched, or an arm around them. Others claim to sense a pat, caress, stroke, or even a kiss – all affectionate, nurturing messages of love.

Liv connected with me through another astonishing event which occurred shortly after her passing.

As I climbed the steps to their empty house I felt my mother's hand on my hip. Liv habitually supported herself in this way as she climbed the stairs.

I spun around *fully expecting to see her*, the sensation felt so real! Their next door neighbor, Sharon, saw me grab my back and thought I injured myself. This time I tangibly *felt* Liv's touch and viscerally reacted to it.

THE REUNION

*When the heart weeps for what it's lost,
the soul rejoices for what it's found.*

— SUFI SAYING

Experiences with our loved ones can occur while in the alpha state of consciousness – as you're falling asleep, waking up, praying or meditating.

I attended an afterlife workshop at the Lifeline Wellness Center where my friend Ellen Hreha works as a chiropractic assistant. The seminar, led by author Karla LaVoie, enabled the participants to create a bridge to their loved ones on the Other Side.

LaVoie penned *For Time and All Eternity: Love Never Dies* after her husband's suicide catapulted her through mysterious and miraculous events that assured her there is no death – merely a change in form.

In order to effect a reunion with those who had passed on, Karla suggested we conjure up a happy memory of our beloved. This recollection would send out a signal to them to meet us in the Garden of Souls.

"YOU CAN DO ANYTHING"

The memory I chose recalled the time my mother and I spent a winter week-end in Lake Placid, New York.

As we drove to the resort town, we listened to a radio interview with Gloria Steinham promoting her book, *Revolution from Within*. Eager to get to a bookstore, I envisioned cozying up with the title in front of the fire at the Mirror Lake Inn.

I was thrilled with the book – it was *exactly* what I needed to read at the time.

During the winter months tiny white lights transform the mountain village into a winter wonderland. The following night we drove around Mirror Lake enjoying the beautiful and magical environs. I shared with Liv how I enjoyed Steinham's writing and my intense desire to write, particularly a self-help book. I lamented that I could never write as well as the celebrated author. My mother replied "You can do anything" – a treasured vote of confidence.

Sure enough this remembrance brought a radiant, smiling Liv to the fore. She stood near hundreds of dazzling blue delphiniums, a meaningful flower for the two of us. With a wave of her hand she directed my attention toward my father, aunts, uncles, grandparents, great-grandparents, great-great grandparents, and on and on. Hundreds of ancestral relatives appeared, each one radiating an indescribable feeling of Love.

The guided meditation continued but I was too overwhelmed by the reunion to continue; I spent all my energy trying to control my emotions.

Ellen sat next to me and I could hear her also trying to control her tears. Later on I learned she reunited with her brother.

A nascent psychic medium herself, Ellen received a message for one of the attendees. A bereaved mother in the audience recognized the connection with her deceased son amid an emotional outburst.

DREAMS

*Six weeks after his death my father appeared to me in a dream…
It was an unforgettable experience, and it forced me for the first time to think about life after death.*

— CARL JUNG, M.D.

Sleep-state after death communications are clear, colorful, intense, and feel more "real" than average dreams. Also, they lack the symbolic language of regular dreams. These compelling dream visitations are termed lucid.

The experience seems as if your loved one is with you in person – as if you are having an actual visit together.

The night my mother passed I didn't want to sleep; it seemed like if I didn't sleep her death wouldn't be real. I stayed awake until after 4:00 a.m. but exhaustion finally gave way. Liv came to me in my dreams.

With five in the family, hot water was a scarce commodity in our old house on Staten Island.

Consequently, when I was little my mother and I shared baths in an old-fashioned, claw-foot tub. I sat behind her and soaped her back and wrote words in the lather. (In retrospect this amusement presaged my love of words and writing).

In the dream visitation the night she transitioned, Liv sat in the tub behind *me* thereby resurrecting an exceedingly meaningful and quite frankly, long-forgotten memory.

Another dream sequence followed that showed us in the cab of a white truck *about to embark on a journey*. My father and brothers and their families stared at us from afar standing behind barriers such as fences and woodpiles.

In life my mother and I did stand alone. As it turns out we did commence on a new expedition together and I ended up writing about our afterlife encounters.

The night of her passing my mother communicated with my brother Jack and her granddaughter Ann Marie via dreams as well as several of my friends. Her way to persuade them to look after me in her absence?

In another lucid dream I observed that my mother set up housekeeping in what appeared to be a small house reminiscent of those found at our favorite haunt, New Hope, Pennsylvania.

Considered the "crossroads of the Revolution," just a few miles north from where George Washington crossed the Delaware River on Christmas Day in 1776, New Hope is a thriving artists' colony. Mom and I shared many happy hours there exploring shops and savoring the scenery.

In this particular dream I saw a house twice. The first time it seemed empty and unkempt. The second time, in the same dream, I saw my mother come out of the tiny house and onto the slate patio now cleanly swept and tidy with flowers. These chores my mother typically would attend to right away upon moving into a new home – as she did to help me when I bought my little cottage.

Liv seemed *thrilled* to see me. In the dream I felt mystified though of course very happy to see her too. A chain-link fence separated us. The fence served as a boundary yet the see-through barrier allowed easy access to my mother. What a message!

There's a related event regarding the significance of New Hope and dreams. In the fallow week between Christmas and the New Year,[3] I felt "summoned" to the town by its discarnate spirits to chronicle paranormal happenings. A subsequent dream further compelled me to write *Haunted New Hope*.

Not knowing that I'd find my mother at death's door, I took the newly designed book cover to the nursing home for her to review on the day of her passing. My mother served as a trusted publishing partner, always carefully reading my manuscripts and reviewing related printed matter prior to going to press.

Despite my heartache, I managed to complete the *Haunted New Hope* manuscript on her birthday, April 3rd, and slated the book for publication on May 14th, Mother's Day. The symbolism of having written about "New Hope" didn't escape me either.

If Liv dwells on the Other Side in a house evocative of those charming homes we so admired in our travels it

---

[3] 2005-2006, just *days* before my father passed and ten weeks before my mother's transition.

comes as no surprise. The possibility fills me with so much joy because she can finally live out her desire.

In a subsequent dream I helped Liv set up a new kitchen. I commented her kitchen looked like mine but then I realized *my kitchen is on the other side.* The "Other Side," in this case, was the earth plane.

Was I visiting with my mother in her new digs in the next dimension? Although no one embodied can *prove* it to be so, many feel our dream or alpha state allows our consciousness to access other realms.

Even after my grandmother "Katie" passed away I often dreamed of her and *felt* we visited. In those special dreams I happened to notice the appearance of a telephone always foreshadowed Katie's coming to me. The representative phone seemed to signify a communication was about to take place.

There is no death only a change in form.

PHONE CALLS FROM THE DEAD

Where there is great love there are always miracles.
— WILLA CATHER

Initially I felt intrigued by Liv's communication. I might have discounted her telepathic communiqués but when she emphatically implored she was **fine**, her words captivated me.

My concern was that hearing my deceased mother's voice might only be wishful thinking or a figment of my imagination.

Exactly one week after my mother passed away, I concentrated on clearing out my parents' house since my father, Edmund, passed 77 days earlier. Their neighbor Sharon stopped by to help.

While keenly aware that my mother's hour of death –

2:35 p.m. – approached, strains of a Simon & Garfunkel CD filled the nearly empty house.

Sharon and I explored the contents of my mother's "button box." Overflowing with old buttons cut from coats, dresses, skirts and shirts, this old metal sugar canister from Norway brimmed with memories. As a little girl I looked forward to rainy days and rummaging through my mother's tin box as a playful pastime.

Their house had stood vacant for over six months, so when the phone rang, it startled me. Who could possibly be calling? Suddenly the atmosphere took on an ethereal quality; events seemed to transpire in slow motion. I heard Simon & Garfunkel singing *Old Friends*. I walked toward the den to answer the telephone.

"Hello? Hello?" No answer. I again became aware of Simon & Garfunkel singing, *"Time it was, and what a time it was, it was..."* **It was** 2:35 P.M.! The *exact* time of my mother's passing one week ago! Astonishing.

I asked Sharon, "How many times did the phone ring?"

"Two."

I dropped onto the couch and allowed a torrent of tears.

The precise timing of the call is extraordinary, along with the "coincidence" of the evocative song lyrics, *and* the number of rings.

My mother didn't always like to answer her phone so we developed a "code" so she would know it was me who was calling – *ring twice*, hang up, and then call back.

Additionally, I had included an excerpt from *Old Friends* on the last page of *Haunted New Hope* as a tribute to my mother.

Phone calls from the dead are phenomena which often occur on significant dates or at times of special meaning. Most often they transpire within the first week of the person's passing.

Liv hit all the buttons with this communiqué and gave me yet another signal of her continued existence and undying love.

Liv took great pride in her home and garden; she loved working in the yard and we often helped each other.

One autumn afternoon as I raked the fallen leaves in my backyard, I *really* missed my mother. Cleaning up the yard was an annual chore we always enjoyed together.

I endured an intense but short-lived sob. Then I heard the phone *ring twice*; the caller ID read "Incomplete Data."

I never saw that message before or since...

Life is not measured by the number of breaths we take but by the moments that take our breath away.

One word frees us of all the weight and pain in life.
That word is love.

— SOPHOCLES

THE MONROE INSTITUTE

Thus all things altered. Nothing dies.
And here and there the unbodied spirit flies.
— OVID

Out-of-body experiences can occur while you are asleep or in a meditative state. During these dramatic episodes, you leave your body and often visit your loved one at the place where they exist.

Much like a lucid dream the occurrence is vivid and intense – some say more *real* than physical life. Typically the environments abound with beautiful flowers and butterflies, colorful bushes and trees, radiant lighting and other ethereal aspects of nature. The event is one of happiness, love and joy.

In April 2007, I found myself drawn to the Monroe Institute in Faber, Virginia nestled in the beautiful Blue Ridge Mountains not far from Charlottesville.

This nonprofit research and educational organization was founded by the late Robert A. Monroe after he experienced perplexing out-of-body experiences in the 1950s.

The institute employs a sound technology called "Hemi-Sync." While isolated in a Controlled Holistic Environment Chamber (CHEC) unit, which has been accurately described as a Pullman berth or the closest thing to a sensory deprivation chamber, individuals listen to a combination of sounds to effect the synchronization of the two hemispheres of the brain which facilitates exploration of different levels of consciousness.

Ancient cultures used the natural power of sound and music to safely influence states of consciousness in religious ceremonies and to promote psychological and physical health. Today the idea of auditory stimulation affecting consciousness is widely accepted.

Not only did I seek further contact with my mother, what appealed to me about the six-day program was the variety of associated benefits such as improvement in relaxation, meditation, stress reduction, pain management, sleep and health. Further studies offered reports of peak experiences, enhanced memory[4], improved creativity, and increased intuition.

Up at daybreak, my daily observance was to contemplatively walk the spiral of a brick labyrinth embedded in the earth.

The labyrinth is a spiritual tool and symbolic of the journey to our own center. Labyrinths have long been used as meditation and prayer tools. At its most basic level the labyrinth is a metaphor for the journey to the center of your deepest self and back out into the world with a broadened understanding of who you are.

When my mother passed, I was bereft spiritually because I failed to nurture myself and attend to my own needs as a caregiver during the last years of my parents'

---

[4] Six months after attending the "Gateway Voyage," I marveled at my ability to memorize the required anatomy information while attending Massage Therapist Certification Training. Fifteen years earlier one of the reasons I left massage school was because I found retaining the required data daunting. Hemi-Sync does seem to work to improve memory!

lives. I felt I needed an intense experience to regain my spiritual equilibrium. So far the "beyond the veil" experiences with Liv led me to question my belief system.

After my first amble through the labyrinth I felt a profound shift of energy which gave me chills; I sensed my protective shell might be starting to crack... intuitively I knew I was in the right place.

At the Monroe Institute, part of the preparation for exploring other levels of consciousness is "resonant tuning," a yoga-like breathing and vocalizing technique which consists of "aum-ing" along with the Om tones resounding through the headphones in the CHEC unit.

The deep, rich sound immediately transported me out of my body.

I sailed over the institute's property and drifted over an otherworldly landscape filled with glowing flowers; the flora was not of this realm. People emerged into view. Although they looked human, they were different. I recognized these individuals as spirit beings peacefully gliding along gently contoured paths.

Next I observed a beautiful wooden door with a rosette-shaped window – like the six-petal rosette design found in the center of the labyrinth at Chartres Cathedral.[5] I quickly passed through one richly-grained door after another and realized I was approaching the centermost depth of my being. Again I journeyed to the center of myself.

Finally the last door opened and there I observed the back of a wooden throne. I knew I would find myself sitting on the chair. Slowly the throne turned to reveal the occupant – a wooden woman! She looked like a tree without bark. Branches served as her arms and legs and roots her feet. At first I thought she had no head but actually her head was slightly askew.

I'm wooden! I was aghast. In some ways I certainly *did* feel stiff. At times I *did* feel life was bleak, after all I was still depressed over losing my mother. In ways my thinking *was* off center – out of whack so to speak.

At first, the sight of my sinewy innermost being left me quite upset. In further processing the experience,

---

[5] In 1970, I visited Chartres Cathedral in France and walked its ancient labyrinth.

however, I realized the "tree woman" was very much alive, organic and strong, yet flexible.

For a year I had leaned on trees in the nearby woods for healing and spiritual replenishment. In fact, I have been in love with trees since childhood when I considered them friends and their branches a refuge. Central to folklore, myth and religion, trees are integral to my life.

In retrospect it's no surprise that symbolically at my core breathes a unique, natural woman whose native environment is the woods. This telescopic journey revived my understanding of who I really am.

"YOU CAN HAVE WHATEVER YOU WANT"

In the next exercise I found myself out in the cosmos, all alone, amid velvety blackness. I tossed out a silent question, *anybody out here?* A lone figure appeared in the distance. When I got closer I realized the person was *me* as a little girl!

Even though I was astonished to see myself as a five-year-old with a ponytail, I asked how I could help her; I sensed she wanted to go fishing.

Mentally I transported us to Eno's Pond County Park. To me, fishing and picnicking go hand in hand. My mother always cut sandwiches in quarters, a Norwegian custom begun by her mother and her mother's mother... I offered the very young Lynda Lee a wedge of a tuna fish sandwich which she eagerly accepted.

"This is how my mommy cuts them."

I knew this only too well. Her statement stirred up memories which brought me to tears. We walked together down a trail and then I offered the juvenile me a piece of Nestlés Crunch bar.

Rarely allowed candy as a child, she looked incredulous as she asked "I can have this?"

"You can have whatever you want" I answered. She looked so adorable and I felt so much love for her, I couldn't resist reaching out and giving her a hug; when I did *she popped into me!*

This encounter also left me feeling as if I retrieved a long, lost part of myself. More importantly, I gave myself permission to enjoy *whatever I wanted.*

During a visit with my mother a few weeks before she passed she said "Now you can have your life back."

Now that she's gone I realize I did restrict my life because of *her* beliefs.

Not only does the deceased retain consciousness, sometimes the survivors achieve a re-birth of their own awareness as I, thankfully, was on the path to doing.

In yet another exercise at Monroe, I watched as an exquisite woman, sheathed in a shimmering, bat-winged dress, descended from "heaven." I thought it was the Blessed Mother, but then I realized I beheld my mother's Higher Self.

Although words are inadequate to describe this beautiful butterfly-like being, her dress radiated with purple, gold and white jewel-like beads. My mother stood beside me in her favorite purple coat as I stood mesmerized by this magnificent creature.

Slowly another similar life form descended, only this one's raiment glowed with the colors of rose, indigo and white. I intuited this being to be *my* Higher Self. Liv revealed that our Higher Selves existed simultaneously and together.

Engraving by Pierre Amédée Varin from *Les Papillons Metamorphoses Terrestres Des Peuples De L'Air*, c. 1852.

CONSCIOUSNESS ENDURES

This mystical conundrum became amplified during a three-day afterlife conference presented by the Academy of Spirituality and Paranormal Studies, Inc. that I attended at DeSales University, Center Valley, Pennsylvania in June, 2007.

At the conference, author Betsy Jo Miller presented her experiences with the afterlife in a program that detailed the death of her 16-year-old son, Kevin. Furthermore, she offered "channeled" insights received from her spiritual guide, Kaju, who ardently affirms "consciousness endures."

Her voluminous book, *The Wisdom of the Gods*, features *some* of the information she has received along with particulars of her incredible life journey.

I sat transfixed when during her presentation Betsy Jo shared that her son informed his mother that their Higher Selves exist together in the other realm. Kaju stated "Tell the others that their Higher Self is also on this realm while that part created *through* their Higher Self is living there."

This stunning information further validated my revelatory incident at Monroe.

The intensity of my experiences at the Monroe Institute expanded my understanding and affected me deeply. I am awed by the Universe, the knowledge of eternity, and the ease of our ability to access other dimensions.

With an open and happy heart, I started the long drive home from Virginia revitalized and well on the road to loving life again.

**Reality may turn out closer to your dreams
than you currently believe.**

HAPPY BIRTHDAY FROM BEYOND

There should be no fear of death, for the death of the body is but a gentle passing to a much freer life.

— HELEN GREAVES

For a while after her passing, my morning ritual consisted of sitting in my sunny den having coffee with my late mother and talking to her photo. Sometimes she answered, sometimes not.

On my birthday, August 18, 2006, *exactly* five months to the day of mom's passing I cozied up with my coffee. Until that morning I didn't give a thought to her knitting basket, which had sat on the floor next to her favorite chair. Today the basket seemed to "call" me so I inspected its contents.

Knitting instructions in her handwriting tugged at my heart. A stray cat toy came into view. Tucked inside a greeting card, with a photo of a beautiful waterfall, were five $20 bills. The sentiment read:

Here are

bright and cheery wishes

And each is meant to say –

You are

Constantly remembered

Every minute of the day.

The unsigned card sent shivers down my spine. My mother always gave me $100 for my birthday, and the waterfall reminded me of one of our favorite places – Buttermilk Falls in New York State's Adirondack Mountains.

What impelled me to look inside the tote *that* day?

WEATHERING THE WINTER & FURTHER SIGNS OF LIFE

In the depth of your hopes and desires lies your silent knowledge of the beyond; and like seeds dreaming beneath the snow your heart dreams of spring. Trust the dreams, for in them is a hidden gate to eternity.

— KAHLIL GIBRAN

After death communications can be symbolic. Their meaning is poignant because the occurrence entails a secret language known only to the recipient.

I planted a dogwood tree on my property in memory of my mother. I even went so far as placing some of her cremated remains in an Irish linen handkerchief, tied with a ribbon, under the root ball. Then I edged the flower bed with white violas, one of my mother's favorite flowers. One morning I went out to the tree and started talking to Liv.

"I'm not there, I'm here," I heard her say.

I inherited all my parents' "things." I placed one of my mother's flowerpots outside my back door. Several viola plants sprouted in the pot. Where did they come from?

Every morning when I went out to feed the last of my feral cat colony, I witnessed the tiny plants' white blooms even during the harsh winter. These little flowers steadfastly bloomed in a strategic place where my mother *knew* I would see them at least four times a day as I passed in and out of my rear door to feed the feline. Another constant remembrance, I suspect.

I'm intrigued viola seeds found their way into my mother's flowerpot... otherworldly intervention? There could be a logical explanation but I believe in miracles. To me that's the stuff life is made of.

Over the years, my mother helped me financially to spay feral cats; their presence in my life was an emotional roller coaster as I recounted in *Kindle Spirits*, my first attempt at self-publishing.

Much like those abandoned animals, we can weather our emotional winters with a little help from our invisible friends.

During the first Reiki Healing Circle I attended after Liv's passing I received a meaningful message.

The Reiki practitioner intuited a woman on the Other Side handing me a nest filled with pale blue robin eggs.

To me, the significance of the bird's nest was whenever I came upon robins' egg shells and empty nests while out walking I regularly brought them to my mother.

As her parents taught her, Liv loved the natural world as much as I do; she taught me all I know about nature, birds and plants. She and I savor life's simple pleasures.

I sensed the bird nest as another symbolic message from Liv conveying the promise of Spring and rebirth.

"NOW YOU CAN HAVE YOUR LIFE BACK"

How can you make denial of Allah, who made you live again when you died, will make you dead again, and then alive again, until you finally return to him?

— THE KORAN [2.28]

As I mentioned earlier, shortly before my mother passed, Liv nonchalantly announced, "Now you can have your life back." Easier said than done.

I lost my parents *and* my interest in writing (not realizing at the time my aversion to composing was only temporary). Feeling totally aimless made my skin crawl, a most unpleasant sensation, and one I never experienced before in my life. Not only did I endure grief, I abhorred the sensation of being adrift without direction.

To get through the days, I subscribed to Shirley MacLaine's website and listened to her archived radio shows featuring experts discussing a myriad of metaphysical topics. I needed to nourish my psyche.

One guest I remembered from MacLaine's television miniseries *Out on a Limb*. Kevin Ryerson is an acclaimed author, expert intuitive, and trance channel in the tradition of Edgar Cayce and Jane Roberts.

In a near panic I set up an appointment for a reading with Kevin; I thought perhaps he could help me get back on track.

Kevin's method entails entering a trance state which allows one or several entities to come through and assist the client. In my case, the spiritual entity, Atun Re came forth. I asked him about my life purpose and why the strong connection with my mother.

The "old Egyptian" shared with me that I lived many lifetimes in Egypt but specifically, the life span affecting the present concerns my existence in Amarna under the reign of Akhenaton.

Akhenaton, an Egyptian pharaoh who reigned about 3,500 years ago, initiated major changes to the ancient culture, most notably in religion. The pharaoh transformed the polytheistic culture to a monotheistic society. Atun, the Sun god, was the one and only god to be worshipped, he decreed.

Needless to say, Akhenaton's 18th dynasty rule was revolutionary. His strange appearance and mysterious behavior, as well as his relationship with Nefertiti and their son, the ill-fated "boy king" Tutankhamen, make him the subject of much controversy.

Atun Re went on to say the man who incarnated as my father in this lifetime made "solar boats," funeral crafts designed for the deceased to navigate the Nile on their final earthly journey. My father (Edmund) excelled in creating solar boats and grew wealthy. Back in those days, he functioned as a godfather to me.

Atun Re said my father felt frustrated in *this* lifetime because although he possessed artistic abilities he considered himself more of a craftsmen and he "experienced disappointments." Incredibly enough my father worked thirty years as a *Ship's Carpenter* for the City of New York.

When Akhenaton pronounced monotheism as the order of the day, the demand for solar boats diminished. Those crafts went "out the window" along with the multitude of gods and goddesses according to Atun Re.

Due to my father's renown and skill in boat building, Akhenaton commissioned him to create ornate pleasure barges. Even so, my father became embittered because his livelihood, and worse, his status in Egyptian society, diminished.

I, on the other hand, flourished as a writer/scribe and celebrated my new freedom. My mother acted as a mentor and "encouraged me in authorship," as she did in this lifetime (!).

I felt guilty because of my godfather's decline while I prospered. Although he lived to a ripe old age, was mummified and received many accolades, my father resented my success *which carried over to this incarnation.*

Atun Re pointed out the parallels of my present incarnation, living through the revolutionary era of the 1960s, which ushered in mass reform in civil liberties, and of course my livelihood as a writer.

Another analogy is I exist at a time when knowledge of a universal source of energy is being expounded. We are on the verge of a psychic revolution, hurtling toward 2012 when predictions include awareness of other dimensions including *telepathic communications* with the deceased!

I resonated with the information Atun Re presented; it evidenced the efficacy of other lives and immortality. The reading also explained the lack of rapport between my father and me and in effect initiated a healing.

Only time will tell which path makes the most sense for you.

"TELL HER I LOVE HER AS MUCH AS SHE LOVED LUCY"

*See now that all of the dark memories of the past
have vanished as the mist before the sun.*

— AUTHOR UNKNOWN

Our loved ones' concern for our health and well-being continues from the Other Side. I'm certain my mother had her hand in bringing new friends into my life.

If my mother could have picked a friend for me, and she may have in this instance, she'd have chosen Ellen – a kindred spirit who reminds me of Liv in a number of ways.

We met at a psychic development class held at Charmed in Company, a metaphysical shop in nearby

Waretown, New Jersey. Innately reclusive, I signed up for the workshop because I realized I needed to reconnect with the outside world.

Besides being unusually intuitive, Ellen is a Reiki Master/Teacher and our association helped me to get my life moving forward again.

One of our first outings was to a Reiki Healing Circle. After the event we stopped for a snack with the other attendees. The topic of "crossing over" ensued and I shared my belief that when we transition *either* our guide(s) or loved one(s) will be there to greet us.

Although still a relative stranger, Ellen instantly received a message from my mother who said *"I'll* be the first," meaning that Liv will be the first one there to welcome me when it's my time.

Although I often heard from my mother, and regularly perceived her presence, communication from my father was nearly nonexistent.

My father, Edmund, passed away two months before Liv in January 2006.

Ed skulked in quite a few of my dreams in which I visited with my mother. I found it annoying because I felt like he intruded on our time together as he often did when alive.

Out of the blue, my friend Phyllis inquired if I was having nightmares about my father. "Not exactly," I told her, but I found his presence in my dreams bothersome. "He wants you to forgive him," she explained "that's why he keeps on showing up."

Other than his presence in my dreams, my father doesn't communicate with me directly as my mother does, but apparently he did manage a message ultimately sent by way of Ellen. "He wants to get through to you," she offered.

"I don't know why he wants to communicate with me now since he didn't want to when he was alive" was my acerbic reply.

While giving me a Reiki treatment, Ellen discerned a low, male voice.

"Tell her I love her as much as she loved Lucy."

Ellen pondered *who's Lucy?*

Again, this time a little louder, the voice repeated "Tell her I love her as much as she loved Lucy."

Suddenly an exasperated woman chimed in, "Lucky! The cat's name was Lucky!"

I knew the exchange had to be my parents; my father's typical mumble and oblivion to the cat's name, my mother's irritation and her need to correct him. And then there was Lucky, my beautiful Maine Coon cat and faithful companion who I loved dearly. He passed away much too young.

It seems as if Ellen and Phyllis were right about my father wanting to get through to me. I felt Ed's unforgettable message was his way of extending an olive branch and persuading me to let go of the past.

We cannot know in advance what lurks in the dark, yet the exploration can prove transformational.

"PLAY TRACK FOUR FOR LANA"

Feeling my way from the darker side, how did I know I would find a guide?
— MEG CHRISTIAN

Ellen received another startling message one morning. A Mark Harris CD was playing when a highlighter pen rolled across her dining room table. Knowing the marker could not move on its own, and sensing a presence she asked, "Who's here?"

"Play track four for Lana," a telepathic voice responded. Not knowing who "Lana" was, she hesitated and questioned *what?*

"Play track four for Lana."

Who is this? she asked.

"It's her mutha." By now Ellen recognized my mother's characteristic Staten Island accent.

Ellen advanced the disc to track four...

During my next visit to her house she told me the story. She didn't know until then that my mother called me "Lana." Listening to the song I couldn't mistake the message. Here are some of the words of Harris' song, *Wish You Were Here,* and Liv's poignant message...

I wanted to tell you how closely I've kept
the memories of you in my heart
and all of the lifetimes that we had to share
Live even though we're apart.

But don't cry for me
'Cause I'm finally free
To run with the angels
On streets made of gold
To listen to stories of saints new and old
To worship our Maker
That's where I'll be
When you finally find me.

I wish you were here, I wish you were here
and all of the dreams that you treasure
Will soon come together
and that's when your sorrow will find tomorrow.

LIV APPEARS

The most beautiful thing we can experience is the mysterious.
— ALBERT EINSTEIN

In the realm of spirit sightings a wide variety of visual experiences exist. Appearances range from a vague, translucent mist to an absolute "solid looking" full-body apparition. Sometimes only a partial image manifests, like the face, or head and shoulders.

Sightings can occur anywhere. Typically the beloved will express their love and well-being with a radiant smile. Invariably, the loved one appears *healed* and *whole* regardless of their cause of death.

Twenty months after my mother's passing, while winding down a visit together with a cup of coffee, Ellen and I sat on my front porch. I noticed an odd look on my friend's face as she held her hand to her mouth.

"What's the matter," I asked her several times without response. "What's wrong?"

Finally, after quite a few moments she said she saw my mother. "I didn't know you two looked so much alike."

Indeed, we do. I *knew* she saw my mother. I asked what she wore.

Ellen mentioned a printed zippered jacket, (my mother often sported a zippered, rose-colored print silk jacket), but mostly she focused on Liv's facial features so similar to mine.

My psychic friend explained that at first she noticed a pink glow next to me and then the luminosity transformed into the image of my mother sitting on the arm of my chair. Liv seemed to be enjoying an afternoon visit with us girls, much as she would have in life.

After Ellen left, I still perceived my mother's presence. For Liv to be with us made sense; my mother and I spent countless hours relaxing on the front porch together and with friends.

"Why can't I see you?" I implored.

"I don't know" my mother replied.

I'LL BE HOME FOR CHRISTMAS

You see, death is not the grave as many people think.
It is another phenomenized form of life.

— EDGAR CAYCE

The holidays tug at my emotional strings as I'm sure is the case for anyone who is without their loved ones.

Whenever Liv would hear the song, *I'll Be Home for Christmas*, she'd always cry. Although I'd never said anything to my mother about it, I found her behavior irksome. *Now* however I get it.

Liv was very proud of her Norwegian ancestry as am I. She fondly reminisced about her maternal grandfather, Karl Marinius Helgeröd, who served as mayor of Horten, Norway, a non-paying, honorary office. Karl's role in

Norway's past appears in history books which particularly pleased Liv.

During Christmastime it's customary to display our family treasures from Norway. While visiting, Ellen practiced psychometry on some of these possessions.

Psychometry is a psychic ability in which a person can sense or "read" the history of an object through touch. The psychic receives impressions from an object by holding it in his/her hands or perhaps touching it to the forehead. These perceived impressions can be images, sounds, smells, tastes or even emotions.

As Ellen offered tidbits about the previous owners of the objects, my mother verified the information through me telepathically. Then I heard a steady stream of requests, "Show her grandfather's bowl. Show her the pictures." One appeal after another, her enthusiasm to share our family history came through excitedly.

Liv seems to enjoy visiting with Ellen and I. She is especially talkative when we are together. Ellen notices that my mother doesn't seem to be interested in our heady metaphysical matter, but when it comes to "girl stuff," Liv is front and center.

ON REFLECTION

The boundaries between life and death are at best shadowy and vague.
Who shall say where one ends and where the other begins?
— EDGAR ALLEN POE

My mother passed away from Alzheimer's disease. During her "altered mental states" it seemed she was on the Other Side visiting with deceased loved ones. I say this because my mother shared information with me that I thought was false or contrived, yet a year later I found the details turned out to be true!

There is no way she could have known what she did unless she was in direct contact with her deceased relatives who she claimed to see.

Psychic George Anderson, who specializes in grief work, asserts that some individuals diagnosed with Alzheimer's regularly pass in and out of the Other Side. They straddle the boundary between the dimensions.

The group of spiritual entities known as Abraham claims that Alzheimer's disease manifests because the individual emotionally desires to leave the earth plane before the body is ready.

As her symptoms intensified, Liv often heard beautiful "celestial music" and from time to time, requested I turn off the radio even though the radio wasn't on.

During a hospital visit, my mother chatted with me as if I was her sister Ruth who passed several years earlier. Liv spoke of seeing their mother and how good she looked, even though my grandmother passed away 24 years ago.

When Liv offered condolences to me (as Ruth) because her nephew Christopher had passed away, I put an end to the pretense.

"Mother, Chris isn't dead," I said.

"He isn't?" She appeared bewildered.

I told her, "I'm Lynda."

"I know!" Liv assured me.

Six months later, after my mother's death, I was walking through a dense cedar forest at Double Trouble

State Park near my home. The atmosphere grew eerily silent and the woods seemed to radiate an ethereal glow.

In the prior week I had chatted with a book store proprietor on Long Beach Island where my cousin Chris owned a real estate office. We shared memories of an earlier, simpler time on the island and I mentioned my relation to Chris and his family.

Since they frequented the shop, the bookseller expressed her sorrow over Chris' sudden death *three years earlier*. Our families were estranged, so news of his untimely passing never reached me.

As I stood on the sodden path, a sudden realization struck me like a thunderbolt. Liv *had knowledge of* Chris' passing because she directly accessed the next dimension in her distorted mental state and visited with her deceased mother, sister and *nephew*.

We need not be afraid, for increasing the light of awareness can help us find our way.

'TIL WE MEET AGAIN

Life is eternal; and Love is immortal; and death is only a horizon; and a horizon is nothing save the limit of our sight.
— ROSSITER WORTHINGTON RAYMOND

Life is a sacred journey. I believe we're spiritual beings made flesh in a physical body.

I *now* believe when a person passes on that's exactly what happens; individuals pass over from our material reality to a spiritual dimension. Their consciousness continues to thrive. I believe they can see and hear us, and their love for us endures.

There is *something* beyond this life.

I continue connecting with my deceased mother, albeit telepathically, often when I'm engaged in doing something we used to enjoy together. She assures me she is "fine." I find comfort, peace and solace in her presence and her words.

Even so, without Liv I feel an emptiness – a void that I doubt will ever be filled. Though I still miss her physical being, Liv's remarkable communication and the knowledge she's still with me prods me to move forward.

Until she passed I didn't realize what a rare mother/daughter relationship we shared. Her descent into Alzheimer's began slowly, and in hindsight, almost imperceptibly. Watching Liv decline and coping with her dementia was my greatest challenge; caring for her, my greatest accomplishment.

My mother realized my pain and that I *needed* to hear from her in order to ease the ache of her loss – she would do *anything* for me as I would for her. I confess that I never knew the real meaning of love nor felt its depth so intensely until after she passed.

Death is a transition into a different kind of relationship with those we love. Strong bonds remain unaffected. We *perceive* a boundary between *here* and *there* only because we *believe* there is a boundary.

I believe Life is eternal that some part of us does live on; there is a spirit world, we are never alone or far from those we love, and there will be a reunion.

After two years, *I* can say "*I'm* fine!" a place I never thought I'd reach. My consciousness is expanded and the course of my life is altered for the better. My cocoon is releasing and perhaps I will soon rise like a butterfly as presaged by the purple magnet's message, which inspired me during my darkest days.

Awakening to the phenomenal discovery of life after death transformed me and expanded my vision of what is possible.

Thanks to the care of good friends, I am enjoying life, having fun and writing. I've recovered because I reclaimed my life, retrieved long forgotten parts of my self and am engaged in pleasurable activities that are meaningful to me.

The future is full of surprises, spiritual gifts, helping others and allowing destiny to unfold with people I'm fated to encounter.

To those on a similar journey I offer this: trust your own experiences and accept them as being real for *you*.

ACKNOWLEDGMENTS

Writing this book was a labor of love in many ways. The project turned out to be a collaborative effort among all my friends who generously shared their time, ideas and encouraging sentiments. I realize how lucky I am to have such dedicated, kind and loving friends.

Without the gentle nudging of Ellen Jean Hreha these stories may have languished in a cluttered drawer and *Array of Hope* would not be so named. Thank you for breathing life into the manuscript as well as *me!*

In the past year, Maryann Way's humor alleviated my grief and drew me out of isolation. How I value Mare's light-hearted approach to life, her suggestion to use the quote on the cover and her eagle eye reading of the manuscript.

Special thanks to my well-read friend Susan Grahn for her erudite editing of the text and discerning remarks which were like icing on the cake.

I appreciate the artistic sensibilities of Pamela and Danny Garber, Ann Marie Peña, Phyllis Sabia, and Robbin Van Pelt in assessing the cover design.

Most importantly, I express gratitude to my parents who endowed me with extraordinary gifts.

I am indebted to my mother for supporting my writing in this life, other lives, and from her new life. *Especially* Liv, thank you for illuminating whatever exists in the Great Beyond.

Also by
LYNDA LEE MACKEN

Adirondack Ghosts

Adirondack Ghosts II

Empire Ghosts

Ghostly Gotham

Ghosts of the Garden State

Ghosts of the Garden State II

Ghosts of the Garden State III

Haunted Baltimore

Haunted Cape May

Haunted History of Staten Island

Haunted Houses of the Hudson Valley

Haunted Long Island

Haunted New Hope

Haunted Salem & Beyond

Leatherstocking Ghosts

Visit the author's website: www.lyndaleemacken.com